I Love Our Earth
Amo nuestra Tierra

Bill Martin Jr. y Michael Sampson
Fotografías de Dan Lipow

Charlesbridge

For Kelley Fincher—B. M.

For Grete Sampson—M. S.

To my daughter Hannah:
I look forward to sharing and exploring
the whole wonderful world with you—D. L.

Para Kelley Fincher—B. M.

Para Grete Sampson—M. S.

Para mi hija Hannah:
Espero que pueda compartir y explorar
contigo todo nuestro maravilloso mundo—D. L.

Published by Charlesbridge
85 Main Street
Watertown, MA 02472
(617) 926-0329
www.charlesbridge.com

Library of Congress Cataloging-in-Publication Data
Martin, Bill, 1916-2004
   [I Love Our Earth Spanish & English]
   I Love Our Earth = Amo nuestra tierra / Bill Martin, Jr., and Michael Sampson ; photographs by
Dan Lipow.
      p. cm.
   ISBN 978-1-58089-556-9 (reinforced for library use)
   ISBN 978-1-58089-557-6 (softcover)
   ISBN 978-1-60734-599-2 (ebook)

1. Earth—Juvenile literature. I. Sampson, Michael R. II. Lipow, Dan, ill. III. Title.
QB631.4.M368 2006
525—dc22   2005006008

Printed in Korea
(hc) 10 9 8 7 6 5 4 3 2 1
(sc) 10 9 8 7 6 5

Type set in Ingone, designed by Robert Schenk, Ingrimayne Type
Color separations by Chroma Graphics, Singapore
Printed by Sung In Printing in Gunpo-Si, Kyonggi-Do, Korea
Production supervision by Brian G. Walker
Designed by Susan Mallory Sherman and Connie Brown

I love our Earth...
Amo nuestra Tierra...

where green grasses
ripple,

*donde las hierbas
verdes se mecen,*

and gray mountains
rise,

*y las montañas
grises se elevan,*

where blue oceans curl,

donde los mares azules se rizan,

and brown deserts
swirl.

*y los desiertos
marrones
serpentean.*

I love our Earth...
Amo nuestra Tierra...

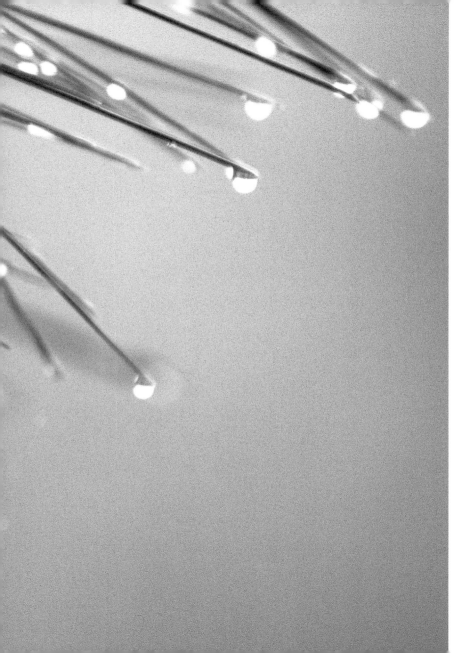

for wet forests
that drip,

*por los bosques
húmedos que
gotean,*

and dry winds
that drift,

*y los vientos secos
que ondean,*

for cool mosses
that grow,

*por los frescos
musgos que crecen,*

and warm sunsets
that glow.

*y los atardeceres
cálidos que
resplandecen.*

I love our Earth . . .
Amo nuestra Tierra . . .

when summer stars flicker,

cuando brillan las estrellas del verano,

and autumn leaves flame,

y las hojas del otoño flamean,

when winter flakes
blow,

*cuando los copos
del invierno vuelan,*

and spring blossoms
show.

*y florecen los retoños
en la primavera.*

I love our Earth!
¡Amo nuestra Tierra!